Cool Careers in
EARTH SCIENCES

SALLY RIDE
SCIENCE

CONTENTS

Kathy

Susan

Harry

Mary Lou

Joaquin

Dawn

Joann

Joshua

Maureen

Adriana

Sid

Tina

What Do You Want to Be?

Is exploring Earth one of your goals?

The good news is that there are many different paths leading there. The people who explore our planet come from many different professions. They include geologists, oceanographers, teachers, physicists, engineers, volcanologists, chemists, and more.

It's never too soon to think about what you want to be. You probably have lots of things that you like to do—maybe you like doing experiments or drawing pictures. Or maybe you like working with numbers or writing stories.

SALLY RIDE
First American Woman in Space
(1951-2012)

The women and men you're about to meet found their careers by doing what they love. As you read this book and do the activities, think about what you like doing. Then follow your interests and see where they take you. You just might find your career, too.

Reach for the stars!

Sally K Ride

On Firm Ground

Kathy encourages students to become leaders in science, technology, engineering, and math. This keeps her on the go—no motion sickness pills required.

KATHY SULLIVAN

National Oceanic and Atmospheric Administration

On the Road

Kathy Sullivan is an explorer. As a young girl, Kathy was good at learning foreign languages. She wanted to travel to far-away places and speak to people in their native tongues. In college, she discovered the life of geologists. "These are people who walk all sorts of crazy parts of the world," she says. "They also sail out to sea and have great adventures."

Ships, Subs, and Shuttles

In college, Kathy spent time aboard ships and submarines. She worked on a team that mapped out part of the ocean floor. Sometimes she endured stormy weather. Kathy's background in geology came in handy when she became an astronaut. From the Shuttle, she photographed Earth's features—from craters and canyons to valleys and volcanoes. She also measured chemicals in the atmosphere.

Kathy was the first American woman to walk in space.

An astronaut flies into space to explore our planet, to conduct experiments, and to study the effects of spaceflight on humans. Kathy investigated Earth's geologic features. Other **astronauts**

* work aboard the International Space Station.
* study phytoplankton in the oceans.
* release or repair satellites.
* explore the effects of weightlessness on the human body.

Frontier Must-Haves

What do oceans and space have in common? First, we've just begun to explore both. Second, whether explorers head down to the ocean bottom or up into orbit, they need many of the same tools and supplies.

Work with a partner and list at least five things you'd need if you were exploring undersea or outer space.

About You

If you could go on an expedition, where would you go? How would you get there? What would you want to study there?

Explore the Explorers

Do some research and write a brief biography of one of the famous explorers below.

* Tenzing Norgay, professional mountaineer
* Robert Ballard, underwater archaeologist
* Sally Ride, first American woman in space
* Sue Hendrickson, fossil hunter
* Sylvia Earle, deep-sea diver

Make sure you answer the basic questions—*who, what, when, where* and *why*.

ATMOSPHERIC CHEMIST

SUSAN SOLOMON
Massachusetts Institute of Technology

Globe Trotter

Susan Solomon's work on the effects of pollution in the atmosphere has taken her to all seven continents. Susan likes working on theories to explain the data she collects. But what she *really* likes is being out in the field—or on an ice sheet.

A World of Numbers

In high school, Susan liked chemistry because it uses a lot of math. In college, one of her professors was studying the gases in Jupiter's colorful striped atmosphere. That's how she was introduced to atmospheric chemistry. "Just the idea that chemistry could be something on a planet instead of in a test tube—now that's exciting!" she says.

Glacial Gal

Somewhere in Antarctica, a glacier is named after Susan. She led a team of scientists to Antarctica in 1986 to solve a mystery. What is causing the hole in the ozone layer over the most southern continent? Susan discovered that the guilty parties are molecules of pollution called CFCs that come from air conditioners, refrigerators, and factories.

"I enjoy feeling like my work is useful. It is closely linked to choices society may make."

An atmospheric chemist

studies the gases and other chemicals in the atmosphere. Susan studies pollution and climate change. Other **atmospheric chemists**

* travel to different parts of the world, collecting air samples.
* analyze gases in a lab.
* study the atmospheres of other planets.
* investigate the global water cycle.

Think About

If you could travel anywhere to study Earth's atmosphere, where would you go?

How can a factory like this one affect Earth's climate?

O All Around

Ozone is made up of three oxygen atoms. Its chemical formula is O_3. The oxygen we breathe is composed of two oxygen atoms—its formula is O_2. Oxygen is part of other gases in our atmosphere. Investigate the formulas for these gases.

* Carbon dioxide
* Water vapor
* Nitrous oxide

CO_2 and You

Nearly everything you do uses energy—from watching TV to washing jeans. Most of this energy comes from fossil fuels such as oil. Burning these fuels adds heat-trapping carbon dioxide (CO_2) to the air. This is making our planet warmer and changing its climate.

In 1958, for every 1 million molecules of air, 315 were carbon dioxide molecules. In 2014, there were 397! The concentration of CO_2 is rising at about 2 ppm (parts per million) per year. Starting with 397 ppm, the amount from 2014, calculate how much CO_2 the air will hold

* in 10 years.
* in 25 years.
* in 50 years.

HARRY YEH
Oregon State University

Rapid Reconnaissance

Asia, 2004. A giant tsunami wave smashes on shore, destroying nearly everything in its path. It kills a quarter million people. Harry Yeh was among the first investigators on the scene. His team investigated over 500 kilometers (300 miles) of coastline. They interviewed survivors. They also collected clues from the disaster area. Harry hopes the data will one day help save lives.

Life Preserver

Early in his career, Harry focused on the physics of waves. But in 1992 he visited the site of a destructive tsunami in Nicaragua. "After I saw the effects on real structures and human beings, my interests expanded," he says. Now he also studies how people and buildings react to these big waves.

Making Waves

How can Harry study a tsunami before it strikes? He creates his own waves in his "laboratory," which is actually a pool. It is the world's largest tsunami wave pool! Harry sets up experiments. He tests the structural designs of mock buildings and bridges as mini-tsunamis hit them. He can even make mini-tsunamis move in slo-mo. Now if only he could slow down the real ones.

Tsunami Wave Basin
COLLEGE OF ENGINEERING • OREGON STATE UNIVERSITY

Experiments with models and mini-tsunamis can help engineers design safer buildings.

A civil engineer designs and builds skyscrapers, bridges, wind turbines, and other structures. Harry investigates how tsunamis affect people and the places they live. Other **civil engineers**

✶ plan and design new highways.

✶ conduct safety inspections of dams.

✶ supervise the earthquake-proofing of old buildings.

✶ restore the ecology of rivers and wetlands.

Here's another wave maker at Oregon State University.

Did U Know?

Earthquakes, volcanic eruptions, and landslides on the ocean floor can all cause tsunamis. These giant waves can speed across the ocean as fast as a jet.

Is It 4 U?

Harry, like other engineers, enjoys

- working on a team.
- solving problems.
- helping people live safely.
- running experiments.

Make a list of what you have in common with Harry. Then discuss with a partner which qualities would make you a good engineer, and why.

Seismic Waves

Big earthquakes can trigger tsunamis that travel fast and far. Suppose an earthquake hits Alaska's Aleutian Islands and starts a tsunami. Imagine the wave is traveling across the Pacific Ocean at 750 kilometers (466 miles) per hour. Calculate how many hours it would take the tsunami to reach each location below. You can use a calculator.

- Hokkaido, Japan—2,900 kilometers (1,802 miles) away
- Kilauea, Hawaii—3,650 kilometers (2,268 miles) away
- Crescent City, California—4,200 kilometers (2,610 miles) away

Check out your answers on page 36.

MARY LOU ZOBACK
Risk Management Solutions

Undercover Killers

What would happen if scientists could forecast earthquakes as they do the weather? Many lives and millions of dollars would be saved. Why can't they? It's because forces that cause earthquakes are deep inside Earth, hidden from us. Mary Lou Zoback uses a variety of data to detect these forces. The data explain how the forces interact with faults and result in fatal shakings of the ground.

Earthshaking Changes

Mary Lou says her field is "on the brink of a huge change." The key is technology. Highly sensitive seismic sensors around the globe send back data in real time via satellite. Now she can predict damage levels while an earthquake is still rocking and rolling!

Surprise Me

Actions that take place underground will always surprise us. Mary Lou found recently that earthquakes can jump from one fault to another. "More often than not, you go looking for one phenomenon, and something else will jump out at you," she says. "That's the fun part of science."

From above, you can see part of the San Andreas Fault in California. It's 1,287 kilometers (800 miles) long.

A seismologist studies seismic waves—waves of energy that move through Earth's crust. Mary Lou studies the risks posed by quakes. Other **seismologists**

✳ search for water underground.

✳ plan for the safe construction of buildings or tunnels.

✳ listen for volcanic eruptions on the ocean floor.

"There's nothing to replace firsthand experience, seeing how science is carried out by scientists, either in a lab or in the field."

Is It 4 U?

Seismologists like Mary Lou travel a lot. They also

- work in the field.
- measure unseen forces.
- investigate mysteries.
- use computers and satellites.

Discuss with a partner if being a seismologist is something you would like to do.

Role Playing

In middle school, Mary Lou's favorite subject was math. What is your favorite subject? Why? Team up with a group of your classmates. Each one of you can share your favorite subject. Then brainstorm together. Could that subject become a specific career, or be important in one? List the careers and the roles this subject would play in each.

Powers of Ten

Scientists measure earthquakes by their magnitude, or how much energy they release. The smallest quake you can feel is about magnitude 2. The largest recorded was 9.5!

Around the world, there are about 130 quakes each year between magnitude 6 and 6.9. But there are 10 times more quakes between 5 and 5.9. For each step down in magnitude, there are

about 10 times the number of quakes. On a separate piece of paper calculate about how many quakes there are each year between these magnitudes.

- 6 and 6.9 (answer—130 quakes)
- 5 and 5.9
- 4 and 4.9
- 3 and 3.9
- 2 and 2.9

Check out your answers on page 36.

"Having a good imagination is important when you're a scientist."

JOAQUIN RUIZ

University of Arizona

Chemistry Calling

Joaquin Ruiz grew up in Mexico City. He was the first in his family to go to college. Joaquin was interested in studying both chemistry and philosophy, until he went exploring with his cousin. "My cousin was using chemistry to tell how old some ancient pyramids were. That fascinated me. I discovered my true calling," Joaquin says.

Rock Detective

Every rock contains chemicals that act like a diary of the rock's history. You just need to know how to read the clues. That's where Joaquin comes in. He's a master rock detective. He analyzes the chemistry of a rock. This helps him figure out how it formed, how old it is, and what happened to it in its lifetime. The world is Joaquin's laboratory. He's traveled the globe, studying why certain chemical elements gather in specific areas. He has studied gold deposits in South Africa—where 40 percent of all the gold in the world is mined. He now lives in Arizona, where there are large deposits of copper. "What interests me is finding out when these deposits formed over the course of Earth's evolution."

Joaquin is surrounded by some of his students at the University of Arizona.

A geochemist studies the chemical makeup of soil and rocks on Earth and other planets. Joaquin uses chemistry to find out the age and history of rocks. Other **geochemists**

* investigate how volcanoes work.
* measure the quality of groundwater.
* monitor chemical changes in Earth's oceans.
* study the rocks on Mars using spacecraft and rovers.

Good Morning, Chemistry

Chemistry is all around you, all the time. In what ways is it part of your life? Think about the short time from when you wake up until you get to school.

From your toothpaste to your transportation, make a list of the chemistry in your morning. Then share your list with a partner.

Think About

Joaquin says, "Being a scientist is one profession where imagination is key." Share with a partner some ways that a good imagination can help you in science.

Penny Chemistry Makes Sense

A chemical called copper oxide often coats old pennies, turning them dull and greenish. Through chemistry, you can make them look new again. Ask your teacher for permission to do this experiment. Don't forget to put on your safety goggles.

* In a glass bowl, stir 5 milliliters (1 teaspoon) of salt into 60 milliliters (¼ cup) of white vinegar.
* Gently drop a dull penny in the liquid and leave it there for 30 seconds.
* Using a clamp, remove the penny and rinse it in water.

Is the coin shiny again? The acidic mixture should have dissolved the copper oxide. There's nothing dull about dull pennies!

DAWN WRIGHT

Oregon State University

Dawn watched Jacques Cousteau explore the seas on TV every week when she was young.

The Ocean Calls

As a young girl, "Deep-sea" Dawn Wright wasn't sure what she wanted to be. Did she want to be an oceanographer, an underwater photographer, or a seagoing adventurer? She was sure she couldn't stay on land. "I grew up in Hawaii and always preferred the ocean," she says.

Hot Spots

Dawn has taken several dives in *Alvin*, a submersible that has been used to explore the *Titanic*. Dawn studies cracks in the ocean floor. These are places where Earth's crust has spread apart and magma oozes out. These cracks often form hydrothermal vents—towers of rock up to 60 meters (200 feet) tall. They spew boiling hot seawater! They're home to some strange sea life, including bacteria, tube worms, and albino crabs.

By the Numbers

"Deep-sea" Dawn could also be nicknamed "Digital" Dawn. Her second passion is using computers to map underwater mountains, valleys, and volcanoes. She pieces together data from submarines and boats. Then she builds a model of what's below the surface.

Alvin can descend 4,500 meters (about 3 miles).

A geographer studies the locations of Earth's features and how people affect and are affected by them. Dawn maps the ocean floor. Other **geographers**

* protect wildlife by managing coastal zones.
* lead outdoor expeditions.
* help developers predict environmental impact.
* guide toxic waste disposal.

About You

Dawn writes computer software that draws maps of the ocean floor. What do you use computers for?

This hydrothermal vent is located deep under the Atlantic Ocean.

Search the Seven Seas

If you're looking for adventure, the ocean is the place to go. More than 70 percent of Earth's surface is underwater. Yet only about 5 percent of the ocean floor has been explored.

It's up to you to explore more. But exploring is not cheap, so you will need a sponsor! Create a proposal to present to a potential sponsor. Be sure to answer these questions.

* *Who* is on your team?
* *What* will you accomplish?
* *When* will you start and finish?
* *Where* will you go?
* *Why* is your mission important?

Floor Facts

Find out more about the ocean floor. Check out its features, such as mountains, trenches, and hydrothermal vents. And look into the life that dwells there.

Team up with a classmate and create a deck of Ocean Floor Fact Cards. Write one fact per card. Illustrations can help to explain the fact. Ocean floor facts make fun flash cards.

GEOPHYSICIST

JoAnn Stock
California Institute of Technology

The Hidden Truth

The job of a geophysicist is tough. Many of the rocks JoAnn Stock studies aren't on the surface, so she must use physics to study what happens deep underground. That challenge really attracted her in school. "There were so many questions that needed to be answered," she says. Today JoAnn measures the gravitational and magnetic fields of rocks. She also sends shock waves into the ground and records their echoes to "see" what is down there.

For the People

JoAnn thinks it's important for geophysicists to help people. Some geophysicists warn people about volcanic eruptions. Some find safer ways to bury nuclear waste. JoAnn often goes on Spanish-language television to talk about earthquakes.

Under the Sea

JoAnn's current interest lies under the sea. She explores where tectonic plates meet, covered by tons of water and sediment. Scientists think they understand the history of the ocean floor, but some areas remain a mystery. Those mysterious areas are where you'll find JoAnn.

Early in her career, JoAnn analyzed the safety of a proposed nuclear waste storage facility.

Sometimes underground forces push molten rock to the surface, such as in volcanic eruptions.

A geophysicist studies the physical structure of Earth. Joann explores places where tectonic plates meet. Other **geophysicists**

* design instruments on satellites that orbit Earth and other planets.
* simulate earthquakes on computers.
* explore the ocean floor in submersibles.
* find safe places to build bridges and buildings.

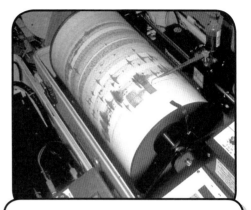

A seismograph is an instrument that measures and records ground motions.

Fault Finders

Geophysicists rely on different tools. A partial list includes airplanes, satellites, boats, submarines, shovels, dynamite, drills, computers, and cameras.

Imagine you're a geophysicist studying volcanoes on land or under the sea. Write a science article describing one of your expeditions. Start your article with a lead—an exciting introduction. Include where you went, and why. Add supporting facts such as some of the tools you used. Conclude with what you learned from your expedition.

4 U 2 Solve Someday

There are many big unanswered questions in geophysics.

• What causes Earth's tectonic plates to move?

• How can we forecast volcanic eruptions and earthquakes?

• How many volcanoes are there on the ocean floor?

• What's the best way to get minerals out of the ground?

Discuss with a partner which question you would like to investigate, and why.

Did U Know?

Scientists use shock waves to map what is underground. That's the same way bats use sonar, or sound waves, to find food and avoid flying into things.

JOSHUA WURMAN

Center for Severe Weather Research

Chasing a Mystery

Meteorologist Joshua Wurman has survived 120 tornadoes, a dozen hurricanes, and countless thunderstorms. It's exciting, but Joshua isn't after thrills. He's collecting data to solve a great meteorology mystery. How do severe storms really work? "We don't know enough yet to make the most useful predictions," Joshua says.

Solving the Mystery

Joshua uses his movable radar to make 3-D storm maps. He hopes to understand tornadoes and hurricanes enough to make predictions. Which will be violent? Where will they strike? "The science is exciting," he says. "Getting the data is amazing!"

Radar to Go

Joshua hopes to improve severe storm predictions with a new radar he's invented. Ordinary weather radar sends one single beam of radio waves to collect information about wind or rainfall. The radar measures the signals reflected back after the beam hits raindrops. Joshua's radar emits six beams, so it collects much more information about storms. It also captures details about the inside of storms. And it fits on a truck, so it can be driven right into them!

Using data from his radar, Joshua can plot which parts of a storm are most destructive.

A meteorologist is a scientist who analyzes, explains, and forecasts the weather and how it affects Earth. Joshua specializes in studying how severe storms form and change over time. **Meteorologists** also

✳ use instruments to describe, measure, and predict daily weather.

✳ monitor satellites that analyze weather systems.

✳ study how human-made pollutants affect the atmosphere.

✳ investigate climate change.

Radar patterns of storms can show wind speed and direction.

About You

Joshua decided to go into meteorology because he wanted to be a pioneer in a field with big, unanswered questions. What mysteries about Earth would you like to solve? Why?

Wild Weather

Good meteorologists know bad weather. For this activity, divide into seven teams. Each team researches one of these severe weather terms, and comes up with a definition, a drawing, and some fun facts.

- Tornado
- Microburst
- Blizzard
- Thunderstorm
- Flash flood
- Haboob
- Monsoon

Next, each team gives a Wild Weather Report, including what they learned about their type of severe weather.

What kind of severe weather event is shown here?

MAUREEN RAYMO
Columbia University

"It's great to do something you love that has an importance beyond yourself."

The Big Crunch

Forty million years ago, something happened that chilled Earth and led to a series of ice ages. At about the same time, India slammed into Asia. That collision crumpled and lifted land to form the Himalayan Mountains. Did the changes on land cause the changes in the climate? While still a college student, Maureen Raymo showed that it did. And get this—she found the clues deep in the ocean.

Underwater Time Line

By taking samples of the ocean floor, Maureen can learn all kinds of things about Earth's history. She learns about its atmosphere, its rocks, and the plants and animals that lived and died over the eons. That's how she discovered the link between the birth of the Himalayas and the change in climate.

The Day After Tomorrow

What changes in climate lie in our future? "Look at the past and try to understand how the climate system works," Maureen says.

Maureen used a drill ship like this one to sample the ocean floor.

A climatologist studies the climate—the average weather over many years—of a region, a country, a continent, or the whole planet. Maureen studies what the climate was like a long time ago. Other **climatologists**

* model the atmosphere with supercomputers.
* collect ice samples from Antarctica.
* study plant and animal extinctions.
* drill sediment cores from the ocean floor.

According to Maureen, the formation of the Himalayan Mountains, the highest mountains on Earth, changed wind and rainfall patterns enough to start an ice age.

Bundling Up

People can put on hats and mittens in a cold climate to stay warm. But what happens to plants and animals? Identify some of the ways living things have adapted to the cold. Choose at least two from the list below. With a partner, name some living things that hibernate, migrate, or go dormant. What are some other ways living things have adapted to the cold?

- Bird
- Fish
- Reptile
- Tree
- Mammal
- Insect

About You

Maureen's dad was a scientist and a naturalist. She followed in his footsteps. In whose footsteps do you want to follow?

Frozen Forest?

Before the last series of ice ages, our planet was so warm that trees grew in Antarctica! What types of plants grow in Antarctica today?

Check out your answers on page 36.

"The Chicxulub Crater has been a fascinating problem, like a detective story, trying to put all the evidence together."

ADRIANA OCAMPO

NASA Jet Propulsion Laboratory

From Dreams to Reality

"My passion from a very young age was to be involved in space somehow," Adriana Ocampo says. After moving from Argentina to the United States at age 14, she joined a science club connected to NASA's Jet Propulsion Laboratory and soon got a summer job there. Now she works there full-time!

Compare and Contrast

Adriana studies the other planets in our solar system. She says we can learn a lot about Earth by looking at our neighbors. For example, scientists study the thick atmosphere and high temperatures on Venus. Why? It helps them better understand the greenhouse effect on our planet.

The Big Bang

Sixty-five million years ago, something killed off the dinosaurs, along with 50 percent of Earth's other species. Adriana and many other scientists think it was an asteroid. Using satellite images, Adriana helped identify a crater, called the Chicxulub Crater. It's more than 161 kilometers (100 miles) wide and hidden under the Yucatan Peninsula of Mexico.

This illustration shows where the asteroid hit and what the impact may have looked like.

A planetary geologist

studies planets, moons, asteroids, and other bodies in our solar system. Adriana compares Earth to other planets. Other **planetary geologists**

✷ design space probes that can visit other planets.

✷ use satellites to study Earth.

✷ become astronauts.

✷ use telescopes to search for planets outside our solar system.

Life on Mars

As a young girl, Adriana liked to draw space colonies. Now it's your turn. Draw a human colony on Mars. First, make a list of some of the requirements, such as food, shelter, and oxygen. Then let your pencil tell the story.

Impact!

Our Moon also has impact craters. Simulating one is a blast. Make sure there's a teacher present and plenty of newspaper covering the area—craters are messy!

- Put about 2.5 centimeters (1 inch) of flour in a pan.
- Cover the flour with a thin layer of cocoa powder or dirt.
- Drop a rock from about one-half meter (about 1.5 feet) above the pan.
- Measure the diameter of the crater.

Make a log, listing the weight of the rock, the height of the drop, and the diameter of the crater. Try changing conditions one at a time—such as different-sized rocks and different heights—and log those, too.

What will these astronauts need to set up a colony on Mars?

Ha-Ha

Q. What is Adriana's favorite drink?

A. Craterade!

Science writing is satisfying stuff. "We get to learn for a living," Sid says.

A Knack for News

Sid always liked explaining science to others. He first taught chemistry and physics to high school students. Then he worked as an aeronautical engineer for the U.S. Air Force. Eager for a new challenge, he enrolled in journalism school. Then he grabbed the chance to write about Earth sciences. "You hope that what you do and how you do it is sparking a better understanding of the world," Sid says.

SID PERKINS
Science News

Covering Planet Earth

Want to tell the world about the hot news about global warming or what's shaking with earthquakes? Then Sid Perkins's job might be "write" for you. Sid writes for a science magazine, reporting on what's new and newsy in Earth sciences. He's covered everything from disappearing rainforests to the discovery that *T. rex* wasn't so fast after all.

Earthbound

Sid likes writing about our home planet. He helps others understand what's going on around them. He's explained the latest trends in tornadoes and discussed our melting glaciers. "Earth science isn't just an abstract thing. It's really about understanding the world around you," Sid says.

Be a Sponge

Want to be a writer? Sid says, "Learn all you can. Everything you learn could help you translate something that's difficult into something that's more understandable."

A science writer writes about scientific discoveries and research. Sid reports on news about Earth science for a weekly magazine. Other **science writers**

* investigate science news for daily newspapers.
* broadcast science news on radio and television.
* write books about science for young people.
* consult on television shows and movies that deal with science.

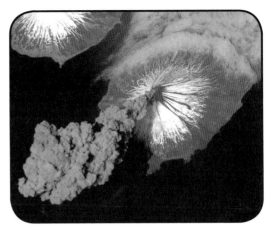

Helpful Words

Science writers often use comparisons to help readers understand science concepts. For example, if you were writing about Earth spinning on its axis, you might compare it to a spinning ball.

Flex your creativity and think up comparisons you might use in writing an article about

- lava pouring out of a volcano.
- a tsunami hitting shore.
- ground cracks on an earthquake fault.
- a 5-centimeter-long (2-inch-long) fossil.

What's This?

The brief caption under a news photo is like a short story that helps explain the picture. It should give readers information that they can't see in the picture.

The image above was taken from the space station. What is it? Discuss it with another student. Then write a caption together. Make sure the caption answers a question or two you had about the picture when you first saw it.

Your Turn

Doing interviews can be an important part of writing. What kind of scientist or engineer would you like to interview? Write down five questions you'd like to ask.

Check out your answers on page 36.

Dangerous Commute to Work

Tina's job is to monitor Alaska's more than 50 active volcanoes from the Alaska Volcano Observatory. The most dangerous part may be getting to the volcanoes. There are no roads. Tina has to take small planes or helicopters to reach her perch on these breathing mountains.

TINA NEAL
United States Geological Survey

In Love with Lava

Early in college, Tina Neal fell in love with geology. She saw the chance to study volcanoes on other planets. But in graduate school, Tina worked on Mount St. Helens during several small eruptions. "That was all I needed to turn my career path into the study of active volcanoes here on Earth," she says.

Be Prepared

Tina has also studied volcanoes in Hawaii. And she's traveled around the world, preparing people in remote villages for earthquakes. The more we know about these natural disasters, the better we can keep people safe. In a battle between you and a volcano, who do you think would win?

Tina studies a collapsed volcano in Alaska.

A volcanologist studies the formation and makeup of volcanoes, lava, and magma on Earth or other planets. Tina monitors volcanoes in Alaska. Other **volcanologists**

* work at NASA and study volcanoes on other planets or moons.
* work for the parks service and teach people about volcanoes.
* study how, why, and where volcanoes form.
* teach at universities.

Is It 4 U?

Volcanologists like Tina work outdoors. They might

- analyze ash and rock.
- monitor active volcanoes.
- teach people about volcanoes.
- take samples of liquid lava.

Discuss with a partner what parts of volcanology you would and wouldn't like, and why.

What's in a Name?

The word *volcano* comes from a tiny volcanic island off the coast of Sicily called Vulcano. The ancient Romans named the island for Vulcan, their god of fire. They believed the island volcano was the chimney of Vulcan's underground workshop.

Composite volcanoes usually erupt with an explosion. This one is no exception.

Peak Form

Volcanologists divide volcanoes into four main kinds.

- Cinder cones
- Composite
- Shield
- Lava domes

Research and create a fact card for each type of volcano.

Which kind of volcano would you like to study? Why?

About Me

The more you know about yourself, the better you'll be able to plan your future. Start an **About Me Journal** so you can investigate your interests, and scout out your skills and strengths.

Record the date in your journal. Then copy each of the 15 statements below, and write down your responses. Revisit your journal a few times a year to find out how you've changed and grown.

1. *These are things I'd like to do someday.*
   Choose from this list, or create your own.

   - Invent new technologies
   - Solve science mysteries
   - Teach people cool things about science
   - Collect data from a natural disaster
   - Travel the world
   - Write computer software
   - Design satellites to orbit Earth
   - Investigate how volcanoes work
   - Study climate change
   - Lead outdoor expeditions

2. *These would be part of the perfect job.*
   Choose from this list, or create your own.

   - Being outdoors
   - Making things
   - Writing
   - Designing a project
   - Observing
   - Being indoors
   - Drawing
   - Investigating
   - Leading others
   - Communicating

3. *These are things that interest me.*
   Here are some of the interests that people in this book had when they were young. They might inspire some ideas for your journal.

   - Traveling far away
   - Speaking foreign languages
   - Studying chemistry
   - Playing in the ocean
   - Taking underwater photos
   - Exploring different types of rocks
   - Observing weather
   - Talking with scientists
   - Doing math
   - Joining a science club
   - Making maps
   - Drawing space colonies
   - Studying volcanoes
   - Building models

4. *These are my favorite subjects in school.*

5. *These are my favorite places to go on field trips.*

6. *These are things I like to investigate in my free time.*

7. *When I work on teams, I like to do this kind of work.*

8. *When I work alone, I like to do this kind of work.*

9. *These are my strengths—in and out of school.*

10. *These things are important to me—in and out of school.*

11. *These are three activities I like to do.*

12. *These are three activities I don't like to do.*

13. *These are three people I admire.*

14. *If I could invite a special guest to school for the day, this is who I'd choose, and why.*

15. *This is my dream career.*

Careers 4 U!

Earth Sciences
Which career is 4 U?

What do you need to do to get there? Do some research and ask some questions. Then, take your ideas about your future—plus inspiration from scientists you've read about—and have a blast mapping out your goals.

On paper or poster board, map your plan. Draw three columns labeled **Middle School**, **High School**, and **College**. Then draw three rows labeled **Classes**, **Electives**, and **Other Activities**. Now, fill in your future.

Don't hold back—reach for the stars!

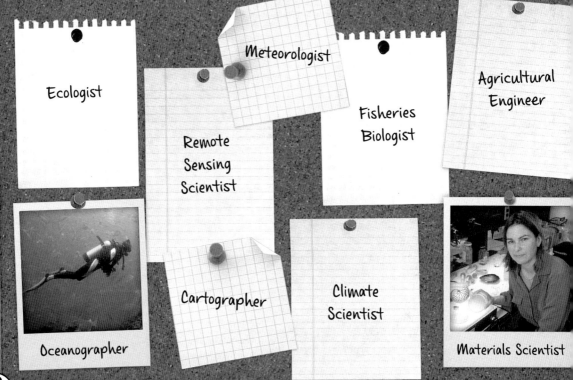

Ecologist

Meteorologist

Remote Sensing Scientist

Fisheries Biologist

Agricultural Engineer

Oceanographer

Cartographer

Climate Scientist

Materials Scientist

Natural
Resources
Manager

Science
Writer

Atmospheric
Chemist

Soil Scientist

Geophysicist

Robotics Engineer

Seismologist

Marine
Biologist

Archaeologist

Hydrologist

Conservation
Biologist

Topographical
Engineer

Computer
Scientist

Energy
Specialist

Volcanologist

Geologist

Forest
Ecologist

Glossary

atmosphere (n.) A layer of gases surrounding a planet or moon, held in place by the force of gravity. (pp. 8, 9, 22, 23, 24)

chemistry (n.) The study of the chemical elements and the ways in which they interact with each other. (pp. 8, 14, 15, 26)

climate (n.) The sum total of weather. The climate is determined over many years and describes what the weather is usually like and what extremes to expect. (pp. 9, 22, 23)

crater (n.) A bowl-shaped depression on the surface of a planet or moon caused by the impact of another body such as an asteroid or comet. (pp. 24, 25)

ecology (n.) The study of the relationships between living organisms and the nonliving environment in which they live. (p. 11)

element (n.) Any substance that exists in its purest chemical form. (p. 14)

engineering (n.) The application of science and mathematics to design and build structures, such as bridges and wind turbines, and products, such as cell phones and biofuels. (p. 6)

fault (n.) A break in Earth's outer layer, or crust, caused by the movement of rocks. (p. 12)

geology (n.) The science of studying rocks to learn about the history and structure of Earth. (pp. 6, 28)

glacier (n.) A mass of ice formed by the accumulation and compaction of snow. Glaciers move slowly downward under their own weight and are constantly replenished. (p. 26)

greenhouse effect (n.) The warming that occurs when certain gases are present in a planet's atmosphere. Visible light from the Sun penetrates the atmosphere of a planet and heats the ground; the warmed ground then radiates infrared radiation—heat—back toward space. If greenhouse gases are present, they absorb some of that infrared radiation, trapping it and making the planet warmer than it would otherwise be. (p. 24)

hydrothermal vent (n.) A crack in the ocean floor that spews out super-hot water that is heated by magma. (p. 17)

journalism (n.) Writing designed for publication in a newspaper or magazine that is usually a direct presentation of facts or events without interpretation. (p. 26)

magma (n.) Molten rock deep beneath Earth's surface. (p. 29)

molecule (n.) A group of two or more atoms held together by chemical bonds. (pp. 8, 9)

pollutant (n.) A substance that is added to the environment—the air, water, or soil—and can lead to harmful effects for living organisms. (p. 21)

radar (n.) Acronym for **RA**dio **D**etection **A**nd **R**anging. A radar bounces radio waves off a distant object, then receives and analyzes the reflected waves to determine the location and speed of the object. (pp. 20, 21)

satellite (n.) An object that orbits another object In space. It also refers to something built to orbit Earth—for example, communications satellites and weather satellites. (pp. 7, 12, 13, 19, 24, 25)

sediment (n.) The loose particles formed by the weathering and erosion of rock. (pp. 18, 23)

tectonic plates (n.) Large sections of Earth's crust that are in constant but very slow motion. (pp. 18, 19)

weightlessness (n.) The condition in which all objects float in space. When an object (or astronaut) is weightless, it seems as though it is not subject to Earth's gravitational pull. But, in fact, it is gravity constantly pulling the object toward the center of Earth that keeps it in orbit. (pp. 7, 21)

Index

CHECK OUT YOUR ANSWERS

ATMOSPHERIC CHEMIST, page 9

O All Around
- Carbon dioxide: CO_2
- Water: H_2O
- Nitrous oxide: N_2O

CO_2 and You
In 10 years—417 parts per million
In 25 years—447 parts per million
In 50 years—497 parts per million

CIVIL ENGINEER, page 11

Seismic Waves
Hokkaido, Japan—

$$2,900 \text{ kilometers} \times \frac{1 \text{ hour}}{750 \text{ kilometers}} = \begin{array}{l} 3 \text{ hours } 52 \text{ minutes} \\ \text{(or about 4 hours)} \end{array}$$

Kilauea, Hawaii—

$$3,650 \text{ kilometers} \times \frac{1 \text{ hour}}{750 \text{ kilometers}} = \begin{array}{l} 4 \text{ hours } 52 \text{ minutes} \\ \text{(or about 5 hours)} \end{array}$$

Crescent City, California—

$$4,200 \text{ kilometers} \times \frac{1 \text{ hour}}{750 \text{ kilometers}} = \begin{array}{l} 5 \text{ hours } 36 \text{ minutes} \\ \text{(or about 6 hours)} \end{array}$$

EARTHQUAKE SEISMOLOGIST, page 13

Powers of Ten
5 and 5.9 (1,300 quakes)
4 and 4.9 (13,000 quakes)
3 and 3.9 (130,000 quakes)
2 and 2.9 (1,300,000 quakes)

PALEOCLIMATOLOGIST, page 23

Frozen Forest?
There are no trees or shrubs, and only two species of flowering plants that grow in Antarctica—Antarctic hair grass and Antarctic pearlwort. The vegetation is mostly made up of low-growing plants such as mosses and liverworts that are able to survive in cold temperatures with little water.

SCIENCE WRITER, page 27

What's This?
Here's the NASA caption:
The eruption of Cleveland Volcano, Aleutian Islands, Alaska is featured in this image photographed from the space station. This image, acquired shortly after the beginning of the eruption, captures the ash plume moving west-southwest from the summit vent.

IMAGE CREDITS

USGS: Cover, p. 3 (Stock), p. 12, p. 18 top, p. 28 bottom, p. 33 (geologist). NASA: p. 2 (Sullivan), p. 5, p. 6 top, p. 6 bottom, p. 7, p. 25 top. Susan Solomon: p. 2 (Solomon), p. 8 (Solomon). Harry Yeh: p. 2 (Yeh). Megan Lacey Zoback: p. 2 (Zoback). FOTOSMITH: p. 2 (Ruiz), p. 14 top. Dawn Wright: p. 2 (Wright), p. 16 top. Joshua Wurman: p. 3 (Wurman), p. 20 top, p. 20 bottom. Maureen Raymo: p. 3 (Raymo), p. 22 top. JPL: p. 3 (Ocampo), p. 24 top. Sid Perkins: p. 3 (Perkins), p. 26 top, p. 26 bottom. Tina Neal: p. 3 (Neal), p. 28 top. Sally Ride Science: p. 4. NOAA: pp. 6-29 (banner), p. 16 bottom, p. 21 top. NSF: p. 8 (penguins). Gary Whitton/iStockphoto.com: p. 9. Oregon State University: p. 10 top, p. 10 bottom, p. 11. Mary Lou Zoback: p. 13. Joaquin Ruiz: p. 14 bottom. Vladimir Wrangel/Shutterstock.com: p. 15. OAR/National Undersea Research Program/NOAA: p. 17. Ammit/Shutterstock.com: p. 18 bottom. Commonwealth of Australia: p. 19. André Klaassen/Shutterstock.com: p. 21 bottom. ConocoPhillips: p. 22 bottom. Earth Sciences and Image Analysis Laboratory/Johnson Space Center: p. 23. Erin Hunter/Sally Ride Science: p. 24 bottom. Pat Rawlings/SAIC/NASA: p. 25 bottom. J.N. Williams/International Space Station 13 Crew/NASA: p. 27. Julien Grondin/Shutterstock.com: p. 29. Clara Lam/SXC: p. 30. Rick Hawkins/SXC: p. 32 (oceanographer). Marsha Miller/UT Austin: p. 32 (materials scientist). Jonathan Werner/SXC: pp. 32-33 (corkboard). David Guglielmo/SXC: pp. 32-33 (graph paper). Kelsey Lost/SXC: pp. 32-33 (notebook paper). Sachin Ghodke/SXC: pp. 32-33 (Polaroid). Alicia Jo McMahan/SXC: p. 33 (soil scientist). Rob Felt/Georgia Institute of Technology: p. 33 (robotics engineer). Jack Dykinga/USDA: p. 33 (hydrologist).